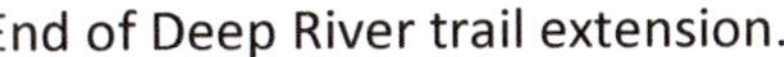

End of Deep River trail extension.

Deep River Rrail - Indian Trail tree.

Deep River Trail.

Deep River Trail.

Deep River Trail - Ancient Fish Weir.

Deep River in the vacinity of Franklinville, NC.

Deep River Trail - Indian Trail Tree.

Franklinville, NC - Ramseur Lake.

Historic Franklinsville Mfg. Company.

Historic Franklinsville Mfg. Company.

Historic Franklinsville Mfg. Company. "Everyone Dies"

Deep River, Franklinville, NC.

Deep River, Franklinville, NC.

Deep River, Franklinville, NC.

Across the Deep River, Franklinville, NC.

Deep River, Franklinville, NC.

Across the Deep River, Franklinville, NC

Deep River, Franklinville, NC.

Deep River, Franklinville, NC.

Frannklinville, NC.

Historic Franklinsville Mfg. Company.

Historic Franklinsville Mfg. Company.

Historic Franklinsville Mfg. Company.

Historic Franklinsville Mfg. Company.

27

Historic Franklinsville Mfg. Company.

Historic Franklinsville Mfg. Company.

Historic Franklinsville Mfg. Company.

CREATIVE CAKES
BEAUTIFUL CAKES
MISC RAMBLING

FLOWER PICTURES
BEAUTIFUL FLOWERS
MISC RAMBLING

RICHMOND VA
CITY OF RICHMOND
MISC RAMBLING

BEAUFORT NC
FORT MACON STATE PARK
MISC RAMBLING

NATCHEZ TRACE
CLASSIC CARS
MISC RAMBLING

NASHVILLE TN
ARCHITECTURE DOWNTOWN
MISC RAMBLING

NASHVILLE TN
LAND BETWEEN THE LAKES
MISC RAMBLING

ANDERSONVILLE NATIONAL HISTORIC SITE
JIMMY CARTER NATIONAL HISTORIC SITE & MORE!
MISC RAMBLING

NC STATE FAIR
2012
MISC RAMBLING

The end.

9 781723 586910